KINGDOM OF FLOWERS

Adult Coloring Book

by Radu Frăsie

50 Different Illustrations

ISBN: 9781073817047

Thank You!

Thanks for buying the Kingdom of Flowers!
I hope you will enjoy coloring all 50 illustrations!

I have a gift for you:

FREE
COLORING PAGES

Visit my website and download all the FREE files uploaded so far:
www.radufrasie.com

QUALITY ASSURANCE

As a quality assurance for you, I offer full video flip through from
my books on my website. In this way, you can see the whole
content of my books before buying them.

Test your colors

You can test your color supplies on this page to see how they react to the paper.
You can place a blank sheet of paper behind the page you are coloring to prevent
the bleed-through to the next page.

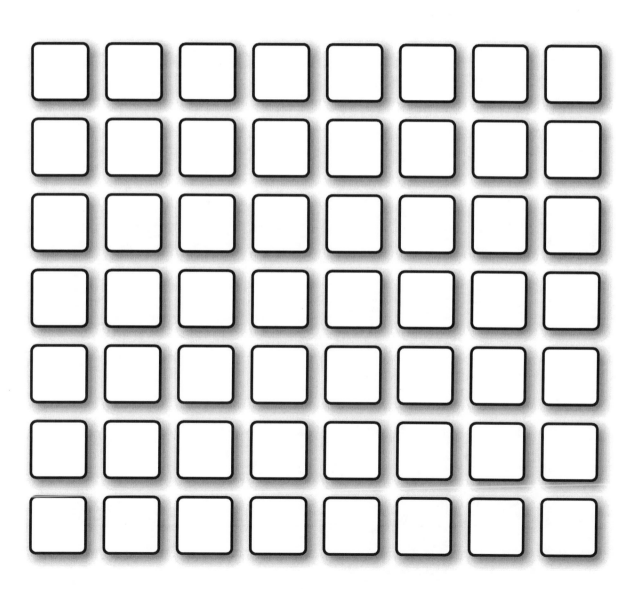

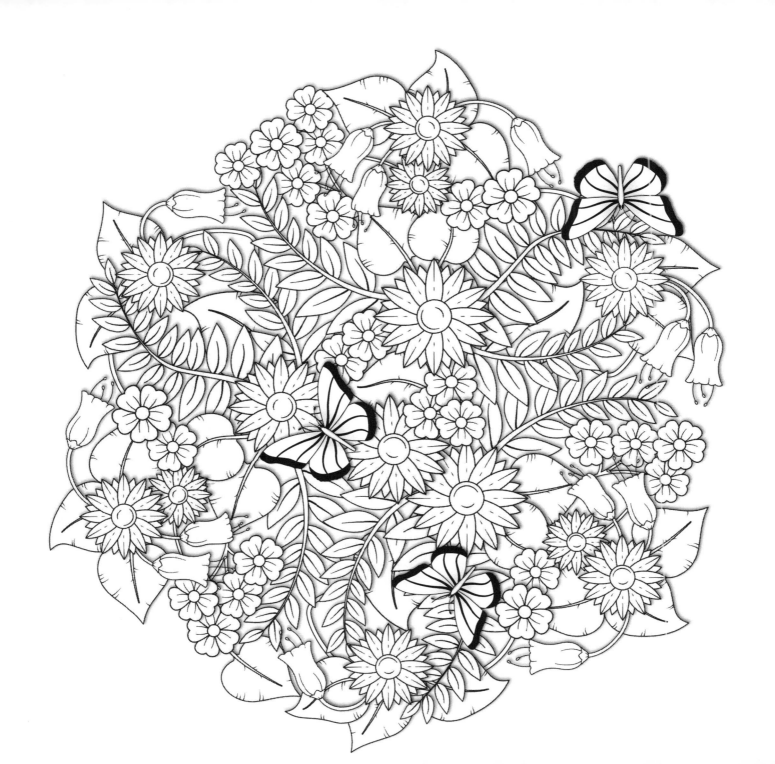

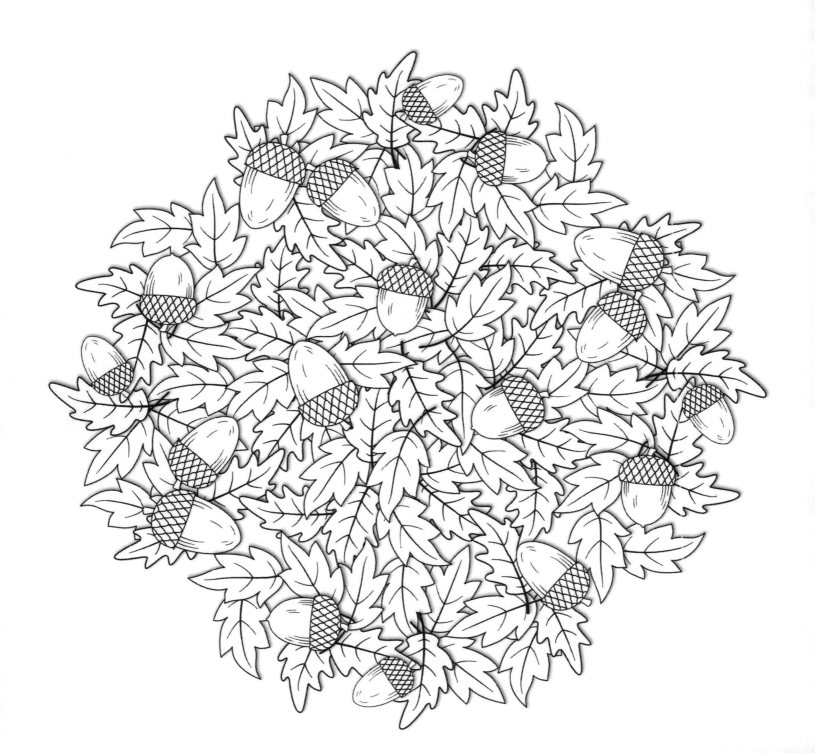

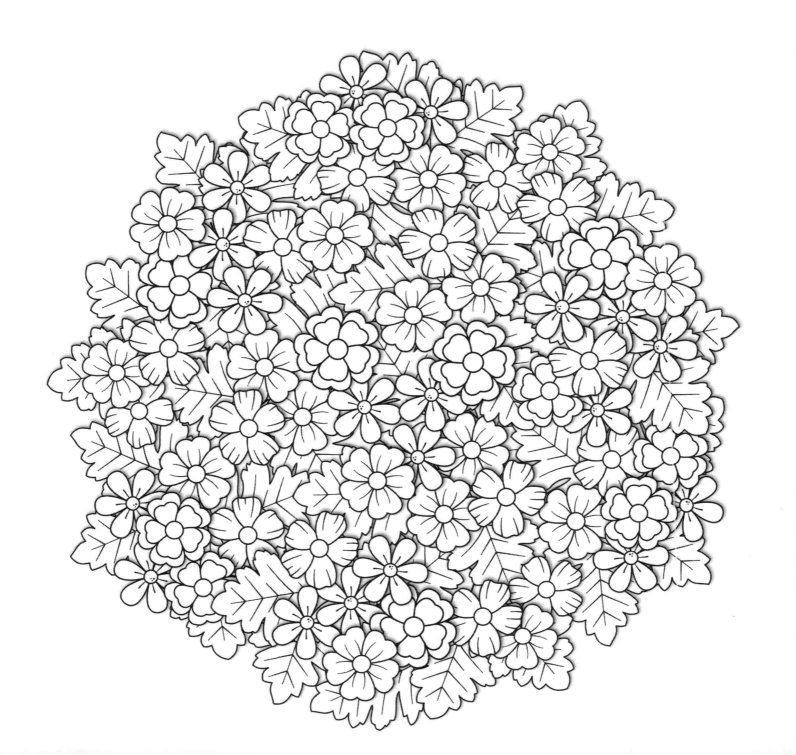

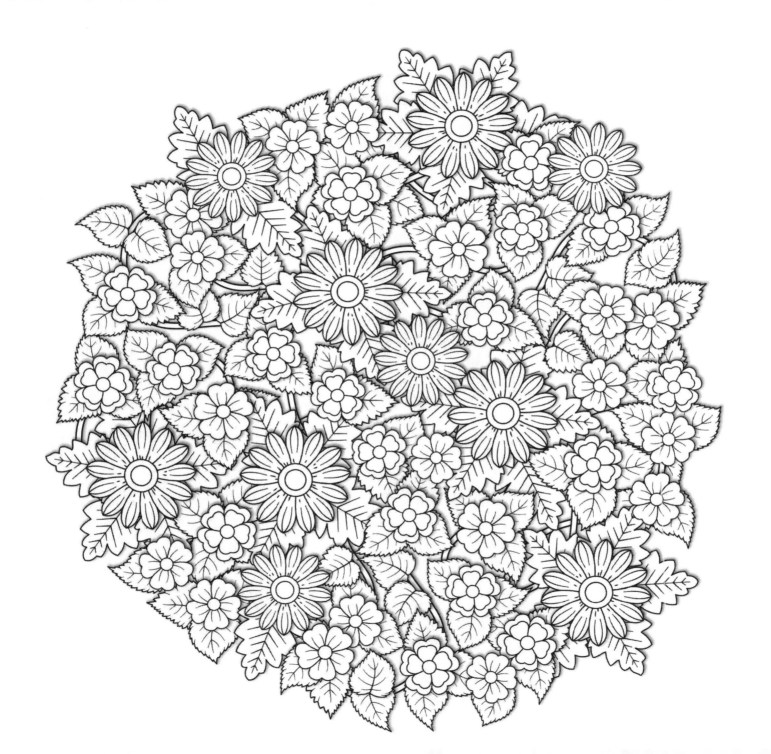

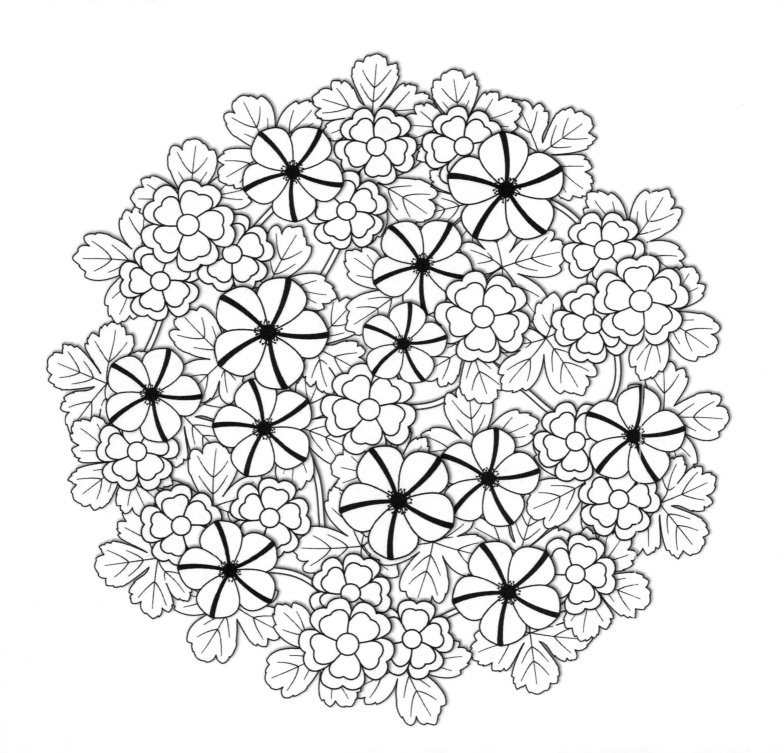

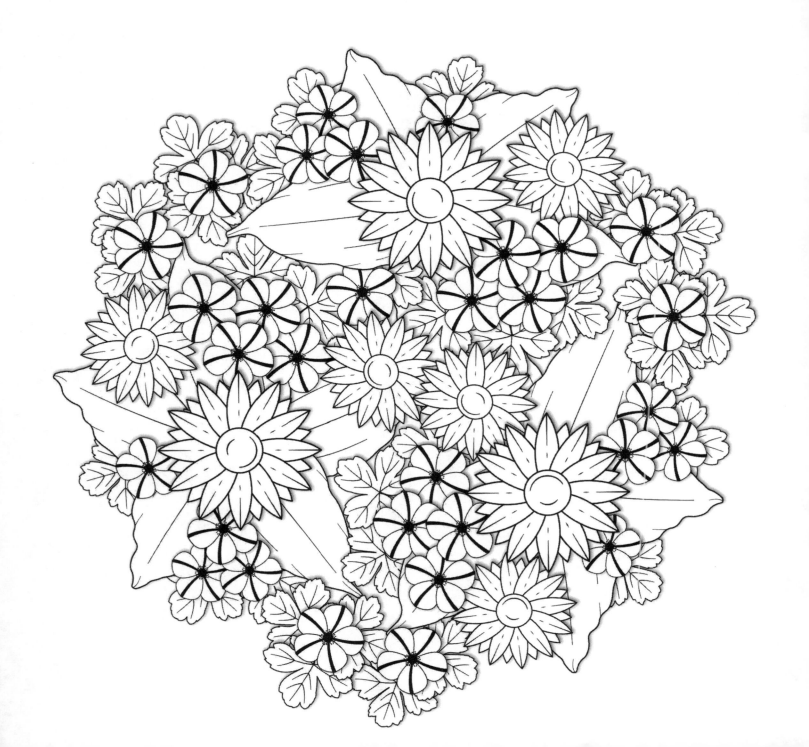

Made in the USA
Middletown, DE
28 January 2023

23023098R00060